amazing ships · amazing ships

AIRCRAFT CARRIERS

JONATHAN SUTHERLAND AND DIANE CANWELL

Gareth Stevens
Publishing

Please visit our web site at: www.garethstevens.com
For a free color catalog describing Gareth Stevens Publishing's list of
high-quality books, call 1-800-542-2595 (USA) or 1-800-387-3178 (Canada).

Library of Congress Cataloging-in-Publication Data

Sutherland, Jonathan.
    Aircraft carriers / Jonathan Sutherland and Diane Canwell.
      p. cm. — (Amazing ships)
    ISBN: 978-0-8368-8376-3 (lib. bdg.)
    1. Aircraft carriers. 2. Naval aviation. I. Canwell, Diane. II. Title.
  V874.S88   2008
  623.825'5—dc22   2007017049

This North American edition first published in 2008 by
Gareth Stevens Publishing
A Weekly Reader® Company
1 Reader's Digest Road
Pleasantville, NY 10570-7000 USA

Copyright © 2008 Amber Books Ltd

Produced by Amber Books Ltd., Bradley's Close,
74–77 White Lion Street, London N1 9PF, U.K.

Project Editor: James Bennett
Copy Editors: Natasha Reed, Chris McNab
Design: Colin Hawes

Gareth Stevens managing editor: Mark Sachner
Gareth Stevens editor: Alan Wachtel
Gareth Stevens art direction: Tammy West
Gareth Stevens production: Jessica Yanke

All illustrations courtesy of Art-Tech/Aerospace

Photo credits:
Art-Tech/Aerospace: 27; Art-Tech/MARS: 25; Cody Images: 5, 7, 9, 20; US DOD: 13, 16, 28-9 (all)

Printed in the United States of America

1 2 3 4 5 6 7 8 9 11 10 09 08 07

HMS Glorious

HMS *Glorious* was originally built as a light **battle cruiser**, but she was turned into an aircraft carrier between 1924 and 1930. By the mid-1930s, Britain had a force of four large aircraft carriers. *Glorious* served in the first two years of World War II, but was sunk by German battleships off Norway in 1940.

The deck was protected by metal armor that was 3 inches (7.62 centimeters) deep.

Hangar area. The ship could carry 48 aircraft.

Main **flight deck**

- When she was first converted, the *Glorious* had two flight decks. The smaller, lower deck was refitted to carry guns between 1935 and 1936. She is illustrated here with one deck.

- As well as having 48 aircraft, she was armed with more than 40 guns.

Control tower

The *Glorious* is shown here with aircraft on its deck. Her aircraft included Fairey Flycatchers and Fairey Swordfish biplanes.

One of 16 antiaircraft guns

Did You Know?

HMS *Glorious* was sunk by the German battleships *Scharnhorst* and *Gneisenau*. Only 45 of the ship's crew members survived, and 1,519 died.

USS Enterprise

The USS *Enterprise* (CV-6) was launched in May 1938. In December 1941, she narrowly avoided destruction when Japan attacked Pearl Harbor. The first raid on Japan by U.S. forces was launched from the *Enterprise*, and she fought in almost every major Pacific sea battle of World War II.

Did You Know?
The *Enterprise* was given 20 battle-star awards during World War II — more than was awarded to any other ship.

Four propeller shafts (two on each side)

Engine rooms. The ship had four Parsons **steam turbines** that generated 120,000 **horsepower.**

Control tower

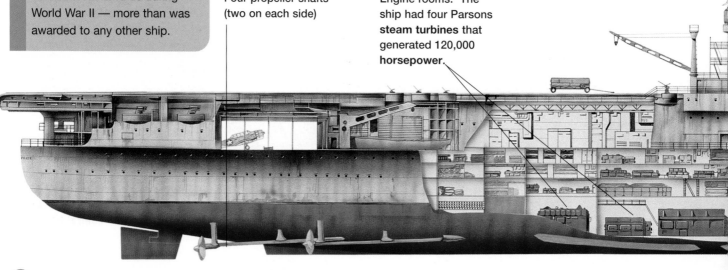

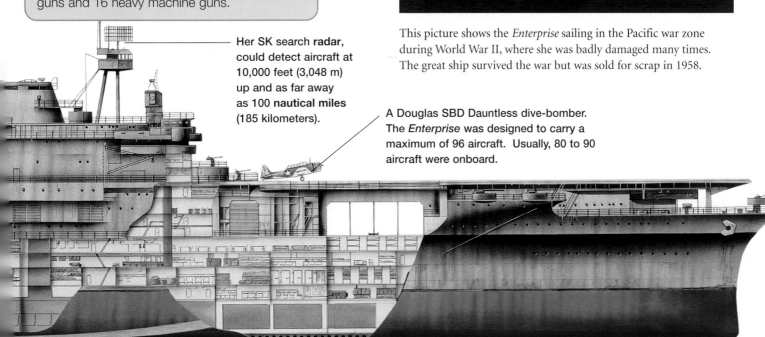

- The *Enterprise* had three elevators for moving aircraft between the below-deck hangars and the flight deck.

- Her total crew during wartime operations was about 2,200 men.

- She was 809 feet (247 meters) long.

- She was armed in 1942 with 12 antiaircraft guns and 16 heavy machine guns.

This picture shows the *Enterprise* sailing in the Pacific war zone during World War II, where she was badly damaged many times. The great ship survived the war but was sold for scrap in 1958.

Her SK search **radar**, could detect aircraft at 10,000 feet (3,048 m) up and as far away as 100 **nautical miles** (185 kilometers).

A Douglas SBD Dauntless dive-bomber. The *Enterprise* was designed to carry a maximum of 96 aircraft. Usually, 80 to 90 aircraft were onboard.

USS LEXINGTON

The USS *Lexington* (CV-16) was put into service in February 1943. She fought in the Pacific region for the last two years of World War II. Her aircraft sunk many Japanese ships and destroyed hundreds of Japanese aircraft. After the war, she was modernized, and from 1969 to 1991, she served as a training carrier for new pilots.

One of the main engines. The *Lexington* had eight boilers and four steam turbines that generated 150,000 horsepower.

Main aircraft hangar

Four propeller shafts (two on each side)

Hellcat naval fighter. The *Lexington* could carry between 90 and 100 aircraft.

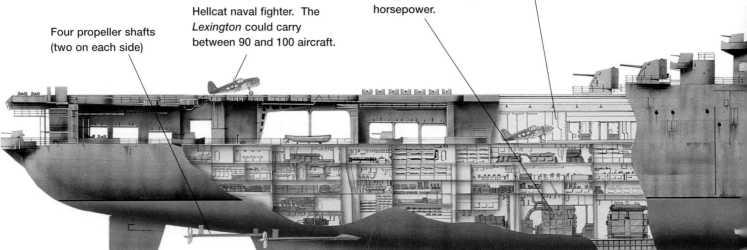

In this picture, the *Lexington* has most of her aircraft displayed on deck. During World War II, U.S. aircraft carriers had a mix of fighters, torpedo-bombers, and dive-bombers.

An antiaircraft gun. The *Lexington* had 8 x 5-inch (200 millimeter) guns, 8 x 1.5-inch (40 mm) quad guns, and 46 x 0.78-inch (20 mm) guns.

A crew cabin. The ship had a crew of 2,600 men.

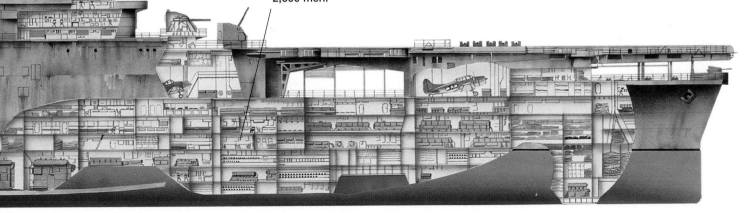

MITSUBISHI A6M2 REISEN

The A6M2 Reisen, or Zero, was the most famous carrier aircraft used by Japan during World War II. It was designed for long patrols over the ocean and was powerfully armed with four machine guns, but it was also small enough to fit into an aircraft carrier's hangar. It played a major part in the attack on Pearl Harbor in 1941. When U.S. fighter pilots first battled the Zero, they often were shot down because the Zero was more maneuverable than their own aircraft.

Based on U.S. carriers like the *Lexington*, the Grumman F6F Hellcat fighter was more than a match for the Zero. In June 1944 alone, Hellcats shot down more than 600 Japanese planes.

KEY FACTS

- The Zero had a maximum speed of 351 miles per hour (565 kilometers per hour) and a range of 710 miles (1,143 km).

- The Americans originally gave the aircraft the code name *Zeke*, but the Japanese nickname Zero stuck, and this is how it is remembered.

Did You Know?

The Zero became less of a threat to U.S. pilots after the Battle of Midway in 1942. By this battle, the United States had begun to use aircraft that could beat the Zero. Also, U.S. forces destroyed four Japanese aircraft carriers in this battle.

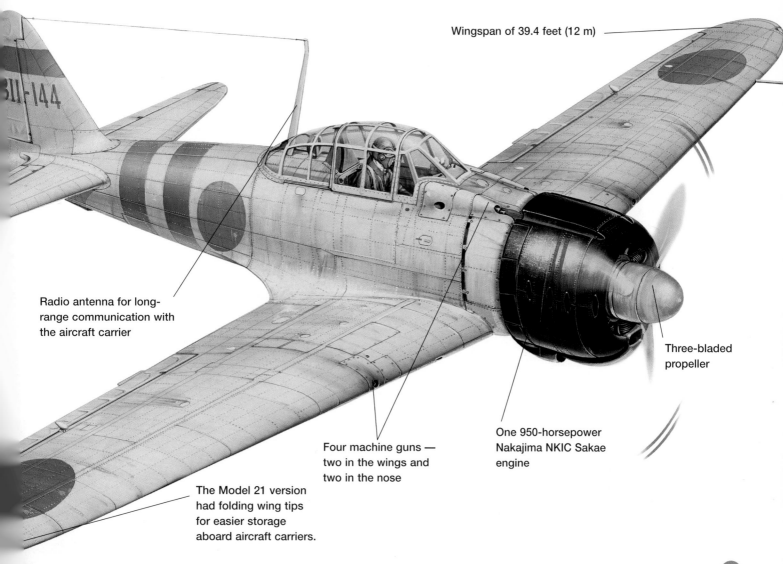

Wingspan of 39.4 feet (12 m)

Radio antenna for long-range communication with the aircraft carrier

Three-bladed propeller

Four machine guns — two in the wings and two in the nose

One 950-horsepower Nakajima NKIC Sakae engine

The Model 21 version had folding wing tips for easier storage aboard aircraft carriers.

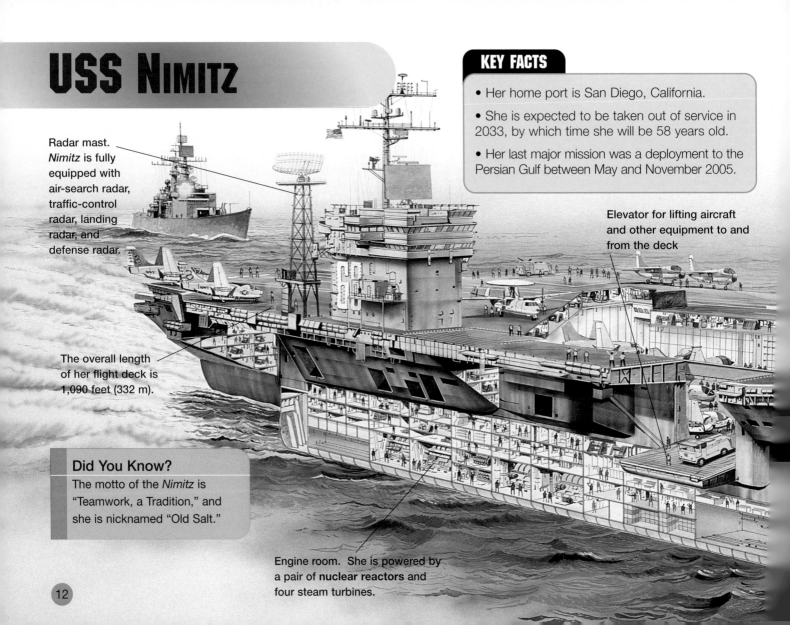

USS NIMITZ

Radar mast. *Nimitz* is fully equipped with air-search radar, traffic-control radar, landing radar, and defense radar.

Elevator for lifting aircraft and other equipment to and from the deck

The overall length of her flight deck is 1,090 feet (332 m).

Did You Know?
The motto of the *Nimitz* is "Teamwork, a Tradition," and she is nicknamed "Old Salt."

Engine room. She is powered by a pair of **nuclear reactors** and four steam turbines.

The USS *Nimitz* (CVN-68) is one of the largest warships in the world. She was named after Chester Nimitz, the World War II commander of the U.S. Pacific Fleet. Since she entered service in 1975, she has served all over the world and in many different conflicts, including in Operation Iraqi Freedom.

The USS *Nimitz* was the first of a class of huge U.S. aircraft carriers. In this picture, a U.S. Marine Corps T-45 Goshawk lands on the flight deck of the USS *Abraham Lincoln*, a Nimitz-class aircraft carrier.

A deck crew. The ship has a crew of 3,200, plus 2,480 air personnel.

The flight deck covers about 4.4 acres (1.8 hectares).

A Grumman Intruder aircraft. *Nimitz* carries up to 90 fixed-wing aircraft and helicopters.

13

F4B Phantom II

As well as being a superb land-based fighter-bomber, the Phantom was one of the best carrier aircraft of the 1960s and 1970s. The Phantom II had massive thrust to help it take off and was strongly built to survive hard landings on a carrier deck. The Phantom II proved itself in combat over Vietnam, where it shot down hundreds of North Vietnamese fighters.

Did You Know?
Phantoms set a total of 16 world records. In one, a Phantom climbed to 29,529 feet (9,000 m) in only 61 seconds.

This symbol means that the crew of this plane has shot down an enemy aircraft.

Pilot

Navigator/ weapons operator

A steam-powered catapult built into the deck pulls a Phantom along on these cables until it reaches a takeoff speed of about 140 **knots** (260 kilometers per hour) in two seconds.

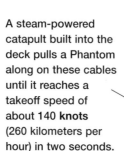

• The first ideas for the Phantom date back to 1954.

• The first fully operational Phantom squadron, UF-121, came into service in October 1961.

• In total, about 649 F4Bs were built.

A pair of General Electric J79-GE-8 **turbojet** engines

The U.S. Navy replaced its Phantoms in the early 1970s with F-14 Tomcats, like the plane shown above. At full speed, the Tomcat could fly at 1,544 miles per hour (2,485 kph).

Total wingspan of 38 feet 5 inches (11.7 m)

The plane can carry weapons weighing up to 18,650 pounds (8,460 kilograms).

USS TARAWA

The USS *Tarawa* was put into service in May 1976. She is classed as an amphibious assault ship (AAS) and is used to deploy landing craft and launch support missions with aircraft and helicopters. After serving in the Pacific fleet, she was deployed in the Gulf War in 1991. She has been in service ever since.

Tarawa's hull is made of steel, but her **superstructure** is aluminum to keep the ship light.

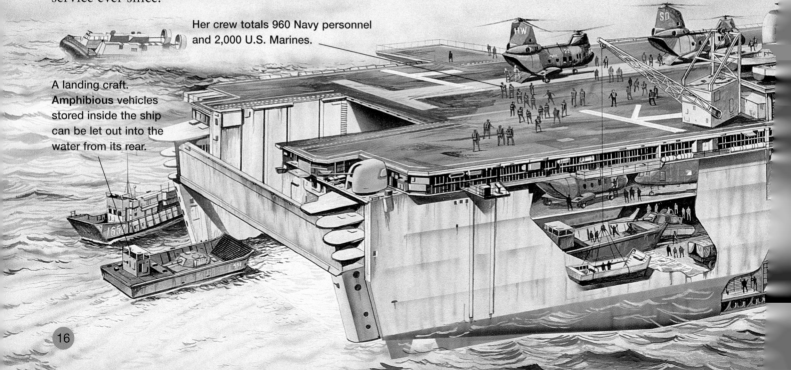

Her crew totals 960 Navy personnel and 2,000 U.S. Marines.

A landing craft. **Amphibious** vehicles stored inside the ship can be let out into the water from its rear.

Chinook CH-46D/E Sea Knight helicopter

AV-8B Harrier attack aircraft

Did You Know?

The *Tarawa* can also act as a medical ship. Onboard, she has a hospital with 300 beds, four surgical operating rooms, and three dental operatories.

Vehicle deck

Landing Craft Air Cushion (LCAC), a U.S. military **hovercraft**

KEY FACTS

• The USS *Tarawa* has an overall length of 820 feet (250 m).

• The ship has nine elevators to help move equipment around within it.

• She is the second USS *Tarawa*. The first was an aircraft carrier built at the end of World War II.

AV-8B Harrier II

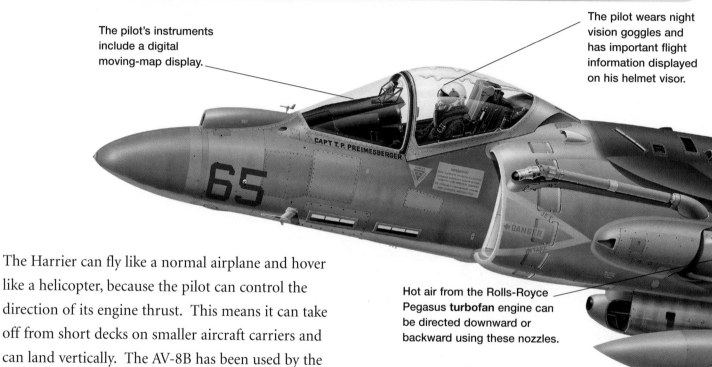

The pilot's instruments include a digital moving-map display.

The pilot wears night vision goggles and has important flight information displayed on his helmet visor.

CAPT. T. P. PREIMESBERGER

65

Hot air from the Rolls-Royce Pegasus **turbofan** engine can be directed downward or backward using these nozzles.

LASER

USMC

US MARINE CORPS

The AGM-65 Maverick air-to-surface missile is guided to its target by a laser beam.

The Harrier can fly like a normal airplane and hover like a helicopter, because the pilot can control the direction of its engine thrust. This means it can take off from short decks on smaller aircraft carriers and can land vertically. The AV-8B has been used by the U.S. Marine Corps since the 1980s. It is an excellent ground-attack aircraft and also a very maneuverable fighter.

- The AV-8B has a maximum range of 900 miles (1,448 km).

- It is slow compared to many other military aircraft, with a maximum speed of about 675 miles per hour (1,086 kph). It can, however, outmaneuver most other aircraft.

The F-18 Hornet is the U.S. Navy's ultimate fighter/bomber aircraft. Unlike the Harrier, it is very fast. It can fly at 1,127 miles per hour (1,813 kph).

This is one of three "hard points" on each wing that are used for holding fuel tanks or weapons.

164558
MARINES
HMM 261
EM
65

Small nozzles in the tail, nose, and wingtips help the pilot control the Harrier while it is hovering.

AIM-9L Sidewinder guided **air-to-air missile**

Did You Know?
In the Falklands War in 1982, British Sea Harriers shot down 31 Argentine jets. Argentine air forces, however, were unable to shoot down a single Harrier.

Ivan Rogov

The *Ivan Rogov* was an amphibious warfare ship (AWS) used by the navy of the Soviet Union. She was launched in 1976 and put into service two years later. She could transport hundreds of troops and dozens of military vehicles and was designed to land them on coastlines through her special doors at the front and rear of the ship. She was the first of three Soviet AWSs built, but only one of these ships, the *Mitrofan Moskalenko*, remains in service. The *Rogov* served until 1994, when she was placed in reserve, until being taken out of service in 1996.

KEY FACTS

- The ship's capacity was 2,500 tons. She carried everything from people to battle tanks.

- The *Ivan Rogov* had a 221-foot x 40-foot (67-m x 12-m) docking bay.

- She had a range of 7,500 miles (12,067 km).

The *Ivan Rogov*'s large doors at the rear of the ship can be clearly seen in this picture. Above them is a large helicopter landing deck marked in white and green.

Bow doors. The doors could be opened to let vehicles or assault boats move in or out of the ship.

Assault landing craft. The ship could carry up to 50 tanks or 80 other armored vehicles.

The design of the *Ivan Rogov* was kept very secret. It was built during the Cold War, during which there was great tension between the Soviet Union and the United States.

Radar system. The ship is packed with electronic devices, including air-defense computers, antiradar devices, and missile-control systems.

The *Ivan Rogov* could carry four KA-29 amphibious assault helicopters.

Air-defense missile system

A Lebed hovercraft. These vehicles can carry two vehicles and 120 troops.

GRUMMAN E-2C HAWKEYE

The E-2C Hawkeye is an airborne early warning command and control aircraft (AEW&C). Its job is to detect enemy aircraft, ships, troops, and vehicles, and report the information back to command centers. It has a radar in a rotating dome, or radome, above its fuselage. E-2Cs fly from aircraft carriers in all kinds of weather, giving U.S. Navy fleets their "eyes in the sky."

Its long wings allow the Hawkeye to land on an aircraft carrier at a slow speed.

One of two Allison T56-A425 turboprop engines

KEY FACTS

• The Hawkeye has a maximum range of about 1,300 nautical miles (2,408 km).

• On a typical mission, the Hawkeye will stay up in the air for up to six hours, reporting on enemy activity and directing attack aircraft to meet any threats.

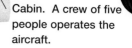

Cabin. A crew of five people operates the aircraft.

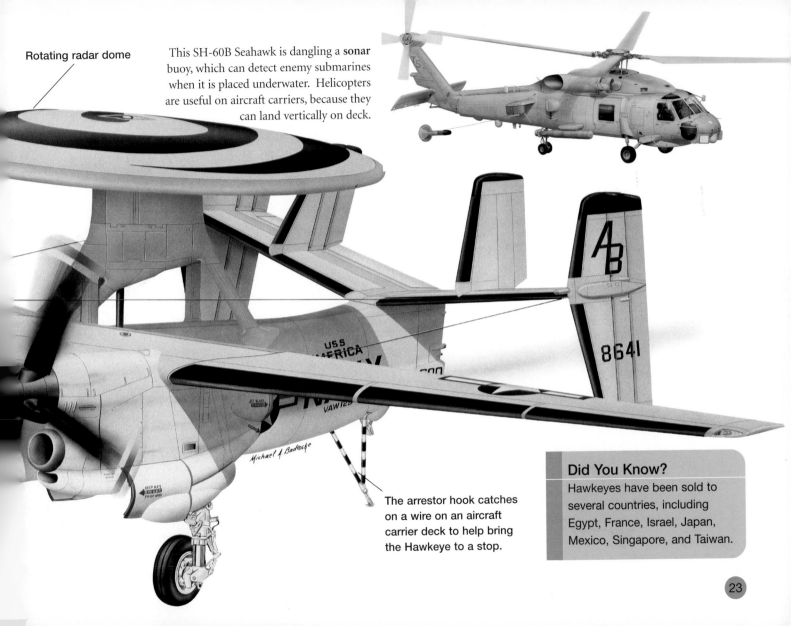

Rotating radar dome

This SH-60B Seahawk is dangling a **sonar** buoy, which can detect enemy submarines when it is placed underwater. Helicopters are useful on aircraft carriers, because they can land vertically on deck.

USS AMERICA

VAW125

8641

The arrestor hook catches on a wire on an aircraft carrier deck to help bring the Hawkeye to a stop.

Did You Know?
Hawkeyes have been sold to several countries, including Egypt, France, Israel, Japan, Mexico, Singapore, and Taiwan.

HMS INVINCIBLE

The HMS *Invincible* is the sixth and most recent British Royal Navy ship to have the name *"Invincible."* Since 2005, she has been mothballed, which means she is not in service but is kept in protective storage. If she were needed for service, it would take 18 months to get her ready for war. She was built at Barrow-in-Furness, England, and launched in 1977. The *Invincible* became famous as the flagship of the British fleet during the war between Britain and Argentina in the Falkland Islands in 1982.

This fire-control radar is used to target enemy aircraft with missiles and guns.

The *Invincible* can carry up to 24 aircraft, such as the Sea King helicopter (left) and the Sea Harrier jet.

Sea Dart missile defense system

A "**ski-jump**" at the end of the flight deck helps aircraft to gain height after take-off.

Did You Know?

The *Invincible* can throw out hundreds of thousands of tiny strips of metal called chaff to confuse the guiding system of a missile coming at it.

This picture shows the *Invincible* with Sea Harriers on her deck. Her maximum speed is 28 knots (56 kph), but she usually cruises at 18 knots (33 kph).

KEY FACTS

• The *Invincible* typically carries 9 Sea Harriers and 12 helicopters.

• She carries 685 sailors plus 366 aircrew. She may also carry an additional 500 Royal Marines.

GARIBALDI

The *Garibaldi* is the flagship of Italy's navy. She is an antisubmarine aircraft carrier. She was built in 1985 and carries out many duties, including watching out for submarines, protecting convoys, transporting commando troops, and providing supplies and equipment to other ships. When she was built, she was the world's smallest aircraft carrier, but now a Thai aircraft carrier, the *Chakri Naruebet*, is smaller.

Radar warning system

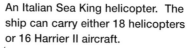

An Italian Sea King helicopter. The ship can carry either 18 helicopters or 16 Harrier II aircraft.

Three-tube torpedo launchers

1.57-inch (40 mm) guns

GIUSEPPE GARIBALDI

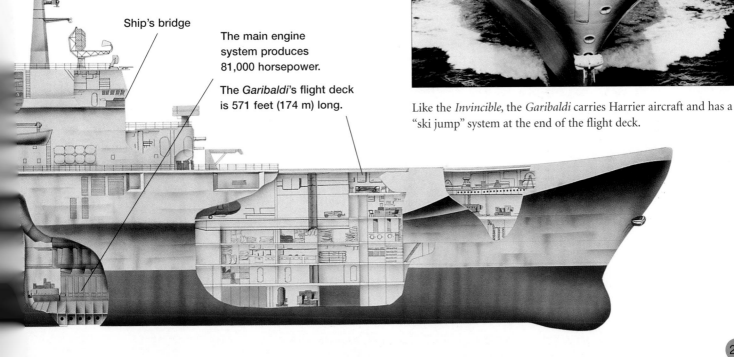

- The *Garibaldi* served in the Arabian Sea in 2001 as part of the international response to the attacks of September 11, 2001.

- The ship's radar system can detect aircraft from 124 miles (200 km) away.

Ship's bridge

The main engine system produces 81,000 horsepower.

The *Garibaldi*'s flight deck is 571 feet (174 m) long.

Like the *Invincible*, the *Garibaldi* carries Harrier aircraft and has a "ski jump" system at the end of the flight deck.

U.S. CARRIER DECK CREWS

Deck crews on U.S. aircraft carriers work in one of the world's noisiest and most dangerous environments. Each part of the deck crew has a specific job. To make it easier to tell crew members' jobs, each deck-crew team wears a different colored jersey.

The chock-and-chain runners, who are reponsible for securing the aircraft, wear brown.

Handlers and elevator operators wear blue. They direct aircraft on the deck and in the hangar.

Safety personnel and landing-signal officers can be spotted in their white shirts.

Did You Know?

The greatest danger to deck-crew members is being blasted by jet engines. The crew members are at risk of being burned or blown off the deck.

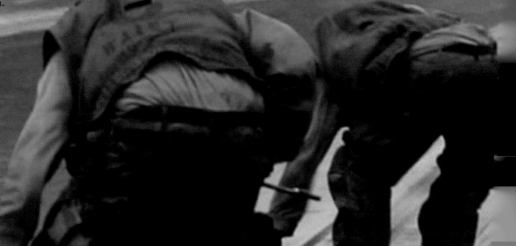

Most of the crew members who are responsible for aircraft weapons wear red jackets.

Members of fuel crews wear purple.

The catapult-and-arrestor-gear officer wears a yellow uniform.

KEY FACTS

- The deck crew operate steam catapults to launch the aircraft. The catapults help push an aircraft from 0 to 165 miles per hour (265 kph) in two seconds.
- A good carrier deck crew will be able to launch two aircraft in less than 40 seconds.

Glossary

air-to-air missile a missile launched by a flying aircraft to destroy another flying aircraft

amphibious having the ability to work on both land and water; amphibious ships can take troops, vehicles, or equipment from the sea onto land

battle cruiser a large warship armed with heavy-caliber guns, and used mainly during the first half of the twentieth century

control tower a tower from which aircraft are directed to take off and land; an aircraft carrier has a control tower on its flight deck

flight deck the flat deck area of an aircraft carrier on which aircraft land and take off

horsepower a unit of measurement for the power of an engine

hovercraft a vehicle that is supported above the surface of land or water by fans that blow downward

knot a unit for measuring the speed of ships, which is equivalent to 1.15 miles per hour (1.8 kph)

nautical mile a unit of measurement for distance at sea that is equal to 1.15 miles (1.8 km)

nuclear reactor a system that uses nuclear reactions to produce electrical power

radar a system that uses microwaves to detect and locate distant objects

ski jump a ramp at the end of a flight deck used by aircraft to gain more height when taking off

sonar a system that uses sound waves to detect objects in the water, such as submarines or boats

steam turbine a type of engine that uses superheated steam to provide power

superstructure all parts of the ship above the main deck

turbofan a high-power jet engine that is used in military aircraft and airliners

turbojet a simple type of jet engine that was one of the first types of jet to be used in aircraft

FOR MORE INFORMATION

BOOKS

- *Aircraft Carriers*. Fighting Forces of the Sea (series). Lynne M. Stone (Rourke Publishing)

- *Aircraft Carriers*. Military Hardware in Action (series). Kevin Doyle (Lerner Publications)

- *Aircraft Carriers: The Nimitiz Class*. Michael Green and Gladys Green (Edge Books)

- *Carrier War: Aircraft Carriers in World War II*. Military Might (series). Tom McGowen (21st Century)

- *The Great Ships*. Patrick O'Brien (Walker Books)

- *The World of Ships*. Philip Wilkinson (Kingfisher)

WEB SITES

- San Diego Aircraft Carrier Museum
  www.midway.org

- Haze Gray and Underway—naval history and photography
  www.hazegray.org

- How Stuff Works—How Aircraft Carriers Work
  www.science.howstuffworks.com/aircraft-carrier.htm

- Warship: Aircraft Carriers
  www.pbs.org/wnet/warship/carriers/index.html

- About: U.S. Military—A Brief History of U.S. Navy Aircraft Carriers
  www.usmilitary.about.com/library/milinfo/navycarriers/bl earlyhistory.htm

Publisher's note to educators and parents:

Our editors have carefully reviewed these Web sites to ensure that they are suitable for children. Many web sites change frequently, however, and we cannot guarantee that a site's future contents will continue to meet our high standards of quality and educational value. Be advised that children should be closely supervised whenever they access the Internet.

INDEX